VEHICLES ON THE JOB

BULLDOZERS

ON THE CONSTRUCTION SITE

by Samantha Bell

Cherry Lake Press

Published in the United States of America
by Cherry Lake Publishing
Ann Arbor, Michigan
www.cherrylakepublishing.com

Reading Adviser: Beth Walker Gambro, MS, Ed., Reading Consultant, Yorkville, IL
Content Adviser: Louis Teel, Professor of Heavy Equipment Operating, Central Arizona College

Photo Credits: © Smileus/Shutterstock, aleksej015/Shutterstock, cover, title page; © Mr. Tempter/Shutterstock, 4; © Radioflash/Shutterstock, 6; © SERGEI PRIMAKOV/Shutterstock, 8; © Yevhen 11/Shutterstock, 10; © Edijs K/Shutterstock, 12; © M2020/Shutterstock, 14; © PRILL/Shutterstock, 16; © Stock Holm/Shutterstock, 18; © aapsky/Shutterstock, 20

Cherry Lake Press is an imprint of Cherry Lake Publishing Group.

Library of Congress Cataloging-in-Publication Data has been filed and is available at catalog.loc.gov

Cherry Lake Press would like to acknowledge the work of the Partnership for 21st Century Learning, a Network of Battelle for Kids. Please visit Battelle for Kids online for more information.

Printed in the United States of America

Note from Publisher: Websites change regularly, and their future contents are outside of our control. Supervise children when conducting any recommended online searches for extended learning opportunities.

TABLE OF CONTENTS

PUSH IT!

A bulldozer is a large tractor. It has a metal **blade**. The blade is made for pushing.

THINK

What do you think a bulldozer can push?

375A
KOMATSU

Bulldozers move heavy loads.

They push down trees. They push dirt. They clear away **rubble**.

THE RIGHT BLADE FOR THE JOB

Some bulldozers have curved blades. They can carry dirt, rocks, sand, or coal.

Some have straight blades. These are called S blades. S blades are used to make the ground even and smooth. Then soil is ready to be **compacted**.

OTHER FEATURES

The **operator** sits in the cab. The operator raises the blade up and down.

Many bulldozers have a ripper in the back. The ripper breaks up the ground.

LOOK

Look at the ripper. How do you think it helps break up the ground?

DOZER POWER!

Most bulldozers move on **tracks**.
The tracks can go on soft ground.
They have great **traction**.

CONNECT

What other vehicles have you seen with tracks? Why do you think they have tracks?

Bulldozers can move through almost anything!

FIND OUT MORE

Go online with an adult to find videos of bulldozers. Write down some things you **see** and **hear**.

Then, write what you **think** about those things. **Make a connection** to something else you know.

Next, write what you **wonder** about bulldozers from the videos. What would you like to learn more about?

GLOSSARY

blade (BLAYD) the flat, sharp-edged part of a tool

compacted (kuhm-PACT-id) closely or firmly packed together

operator (AH-puh-ray-tuhr) someone who works a machine

rubble (RUH-buhl) broken pieces of stone, brick, or concrete

tracks (TRAKS) the metal or rubber belts on a vehicle that make it move

traction (TRAK-shuhn) the force that causes a moving thing to grip a surface

INDEX

ABOUT THE AUTHOR

Samantha Bell has written over 100 books for children. She lives in South Carolina with her family and pets.